for The Scholars

FIVE TRADITIONAL S

arranged by JOHN RUT

1. THE GIRL I LEFT BEHIND ME

Irish

* or other suitable syllable

Printed in Great Britain

OXFORD UNIVERSITY PRESS, MUSIC DEPARTMENT, GREAT CLARENDON STREET, OXFORD OX2 6DP

mp
pah pah pah pah pah pah
pah pah pah pah pah pah pah pah pah pah pah pah
heart do fill Since part-ing from my Sal - ly; I seek no more the fine and gay, For each doth but re -
pah pah pah pah pah bom bom bom bom bom bom
bom bom bom bom bom
f
pah pah pah pah pah pah pah pah I seek no more the
pah pah pah pah pah pah pah pah I seek no more the
- mind me How swift-ly passed the hours a-way With the girl I left be - hind me. I seek no more the
bom bom bom pah pah pah pah pah pah pah. I seek no more the
bom bom bom bom bom bom bom bom. I seek no more the
p
fine and gay, For each doth but re - mind me How swift-ly passed the hours a - way With the
fine and gay, For each doth but re - mind me the hours a - way
fine and gay, For each doth but re - mind me How swift-ly passed the hours a - way With the
fine and gay, For each doth but re - mind me How swift-ly passed the hours a - way With the
fine and gay, For each doth but re - mind me the hours a - way With the

p legato
girl I left be - hind me.
Ah
mp espress.
p
Ah
Ah
mp espress.
girl I left be - hind me.
2. O ne'er shall I for - get that night— The
legato
girl be - hind me.
Ah
Ah
girl be - hind me.
Ah
S.
A.
Ah
T.
stars were bright a - bove me, And gent - ly lent their sil - v'ry light When first she vow'd to
Bar.
Ah
B.
poco rubato
mp
p
Ah
Ah
mf
p
love me. But now I'm bound to Bright-on camp; Kind hea-ven then pray guide me, And bring me safe-ly
mp
p
Ah
Ah
mp
p
Ah
Ah

Tempo giusto
mf poco legato
back a - gain To the girl I left be - hind me. But now I'm bound to Bright-on camp, Kind
But now I'm bound to Bright-on camp, Kind
But now I'm bound to Bright-on camp, Kind
Soprano only
mf leggiero
3. Her
heaven then pray guide me, And bring me safe-ly back a-gain To the girl I left be - hind me.
hea-ven then pray guide me, And bring me back a-gain To the girl be - hind me.
hea-ven then pray guide me, And bring me back a-gain To the girl be - hind me.
S.
A.
T.
Bar.
B.
gol-den hair in ring-lets fair, Her eyes like diamonds shining, Her slen-der waist, with carr-iage chaste, May
Her hair in ringlets fair, Her eyes like dia-monds shin-ing, her waist, with carr-iage chaste, May
Her hair in ringlets fair, Her eyes like dia-monds shin-ing, her waist, with carr-iage chaste, May

(mf)
leave the swain re-pin - ing. Ye Gods, O hear my prayer! To my fair to bind — me,
(mf)
leave re - pin - ing. Ye Gods, O hear my prayer! To my fair to bind — me,
f
leave re - pin - ing. Ye Gods a-bove! O hear my prayer, To my beau-teous fair to bind me, And
f
Ye Gods a-bove! O hear my prayer, To my beau-teous fair to bind — me,
f
Ye Gods a-bove! O hear my prayer, To my beau-teous fair to bind me,
ff
And send me back a-gain To the girl I — left be-hind me. Ye Gods a-bove! O hear my prayer, To my
ff
And send me back a-gain To the girl be - hind me. Ye Gods a-bove! O hear my prayer, To my
ff
send me safe-ly back a-gain To the girl I left be - hind me. Ye Gods a-bove! O hear my prayer, To my
ff
And send me back a-gain To the girl I left be - hind me. Ye Gods a-bove! O hear my prayer, To my
ff
And send me back a-gain To the girl be - hind me. Ye Gods a - bove! O hear my prayer, To my
Largamente
A tempo
Whistle
beau-teous fair to bind me, And send me safe-ly home a-gain.
Whistle
beau-teous fair to bind — me safe - ly home a - gain
p
beau-teous fair to bind me, And send me safe- ly home a-gain. pom pom pom
p
beau-teous fair to bind — me, And send me safe-ly home a - gain. pom pom pom
p
beau-teous fair to bind — me a - gain. pom pom pom

2. O WALY, WALY

Somerset

mp
oak Think-ing that he was a trus-ty tree; But first he bend-ed and then he
mp
oak Think-ing that he was a trus-ty tree; he bend-ed
mp
-gainst some oak Think-ing that he was a trus-ty tree; But first he bend-ed and then he
mp
oak Think-ing that he was a trus-ty tree; he bend-ed
mp
-gainst some oak Think-ing that he was a trus-ty tree; he bend-ed
mf dim. mp dolce
broke; And so did my false love to me. 4. A ship there
mf dim. p legato
broke, my false love to me. (Hum)
mf dim. p legato
broke; And so did my false love to me. (Hum)
mf dim. p legato
broke, my false love to me. (Hum)
mf dim. p legato
broke, my false love to me. (Hum)
is and she sails the sea, She's load-ed deep as deep can be, But not so

mp
deep as the love I'm in: I know not if I sink or swim.
mp
Ah
p
5. O love is hand - some and love is fine, And love's a jew - el while it is
pp
p
mp
pp
p
cresc.
pp
p
cresc.
(Hum)
pp
p
cresc.
pp
new, But when it is old it grow-eth cold, And fades a - way like morn-ing dew.
p dim.
pp niente
p dim.
pp niente
p dim.
pp niente
p dim.
pp niente

3. THE BRITISH GRENADIERS

S.
A.
T.
Bar.
B.
cresc.
pa pa pa pa pa pa pa pa pa pa pa pa pa pa pa
pa pa pa pa pa pa pa pa pa pa pa pa pa pa pa
pare, With a tow row row row row row row To the Bri - tish Gre - na - diers.
pare, With a tow row row row row row row To the Bri - tish Gre - na - diers.
brmm
mf
pa Some talk of Al - ex - an - der And some of Her - cu - les, Of Hec - tor and Ly-
pa Some talk of Al - ex - an - der And some of Her - cu - les, Of Hec - tor and Ly-
Some talk of Al - ex - an - der And some of Her - cu - les, Of Hec - tor and Ly-
pa pa pa brmm brmm brmm brmm brmm brmm brmm brmm brmm brmm
brmm brmm brmm brmm brmm brmm brmm brmm brmm brmm
f
- san - der And such great names as these; But of all the world's brave he - roes There's
- san - der And such great names as these; But of all the world's brave he - roes There's
- san - der And such great names as these; But of all the world's brave he - roes There's
Bar. B.
brmm brmm brmm brmm brmm brmm brmm brmm brmm brmm

dim. mp cresc. mf
none that can com - pare, With a tow row row row row row row To the Bri-tish Gre-na - diers.
dim. mp cresc. mf
none that can com- pare, Tow row row row To the Bri-tish Gre-na - diers.
mf f
none that can com - pare, With a tow row row To the British Gre-na- diers. 2. When-
dim. mp cresc. mf f
brmm brmm brmm brmm brmm brmm brmm brmm brmm brmm brmm 2. When-
S.
A.
T.
Bar.
B.
f
Pa pa pa pa pa pa pa pa pa pa
f
Pa pa pa pa pa pa pa pa pa pa
- e'er we are com - mand-ed To storm the pal - i - sades, Our lead-ers march with
- e'er we are com - mand-ed To storm the pal - i - sades, Our lead-ers march with
- e'er we are com- mand-ed To storm the pal - i - sades, Our lead-ers march with
3
pa pa pa pa pa pa pa pa pa pa
3
pa pa pa pa pa pa pa pa pa pa pa pa pa pa
fus - es And we with hand gre - nades; We throw them from the gla - cis A-
fus - es And we with hand gre - nades; We throw them from the gla - cis A-
fus - es And we with hand gre - nades; We throw them from the gla - cis A-

mf
pa pa pa pa pa pa
mf
pa pa pa pa pa pa
mf cresc. f
- bout the e - ne-mies' ears; Sing tow row row row row row row, The Bri - tish Gre - na -
mf cresc. f
- bout the e - ne-mies' ears; Sing tow row row, The Bri - tish Gre - na -
f
- bout the e - ne-mies' ears; The Bri - tish Gre - na -
f
3. Then let us fill a bump - er And drink a health to those Who car-ry caps and
f
3. Then let us fill a bump - er And drink a health to those Who car-ry caps and
- diers. 3. Then let us fill a bump - er And drink a health to those Who car-ry caps and
- diers. 3. Then let us fill a bump - er And drink a health to those Who car-ry caps and
- diers. 3. Then let us fill a bump - er And drink a health to those Who car-ry caps and
ff
pouch - es And wear the loup - èd clothes. May they Live
ff
pouch - es And wear the loup - èd clothes. May they and their com - mand - ers Live
ff
pouch - es And wear the loup - èd clothes. May they Live
ff
pouch - es And wear the loup - èd clothes. May they and their com - mand - ers Live
ff
pouch - es And wear the loup - èd clothes. May they and their com - mand - ers Live

mp cresc.
hap-py all their years, With a tow row row row row row row row row row row row
mp cresc.
hap-py all their years, With a tow row row row row row row row
f cresc.
hap-py all their years, With a tow row
p cresc. f cresc.
hap-py all their years, With a tow row row row row row row row row, with a
mf cresc.
hap-py all their years, With a tow row
ff Largamente A tempo dim. p
row row row For the Bri-tish Gre-na-diers.
ff dim. p
row row row For the Bri-tish Gre-na-diers. pa pa pa pa pa pa pa
ff dim. p
row row row For the Bri-tish Gre-na-diers. pa pa pa pa pa pa pa pa
ff dim. p
row row row For the Bri-tish Gre-na-diers. brmm brmm brmm brmm brmm
ff dim. p
row row row For the Bri-tish Gre-na-diers. brmm brmm brmm brmm brmm
rit. a niente
p pp
pa pa pa pa pa pa pa pa pa
pp a ni-ente
pa pa pa pa pa pa pa
pp a ni-ente
pa pa pa pa pa pa pa
pp a niente
brmm brmm brmm brmm brmm brmm brmm brmm (mm)
pp a niente
brmm brmm brmm brmm brmm brmm brmm brmm (mm)

4. GOLDEN SLUMBERS

17th-century words

mf cantabile
Gol - den slum - bers kiss your eyes; Smiles a - wake you when you
Gol - den slum - bers kiss your eyes; Smiles a - wake you when you
Gol - den slum - bers kiss your eyes; Smiles a - wake you when you
Gol - den slum - bers kiss your eyes; Smiles a - wake you when you
dim.
p
mp
Sleep, pret - ty wan - tons, do not cry, And I will
rise; Sleep, wan - tons, do not cry, I will
rise; Sleep, pret - ty wan - tons, do not cry, I will
rise; And I will
rise; Sleep pret - ty wan - tons, do not cry, And I will
sing a lul - la - by.
sing a lul - la - by. Lul - la - by, lul - la - by, lul - la - by.
sing a lul - la - by, lul - la - by.
sing a lul - la - by. Lul - la - by, lul - la - by, lul - la - by.
mf dolce
sing a lul - la - by. Care you

mp
Lul - la - by, lul - la - by. Lul - la - by, lul - la -
mp
Lul - la - by, lul - la - by. Lul - la - by, lul - la -
mp
Lul - la - by, lul - la - by. Lul - la - by, lul - la -
know not, there - fore sleep, While I o'er you watch do
mp
Sleep, pret - ty dar - lings, do not cry, And I will
p
dim.
- by. Lul - la - by, lul - la - by, lul -
p
dim.
- by. Lul - la - by, lul - la - by, lul -
p
dim.
- by. Lul - la - by, lul - la - by, lul -
p
keep; Lul - la, lul - la - by, lul - la -
rit.
sing a lul - la - by.
dim.
pp
- la - by, lul - la - by, lul - la - by, lul - la - by.
dim.
pp
- la - by, lul - la - by, lul - la - by, lul - la - by.
dim.
pp
- la, lul - la - by, lul - la - by.
dim.
pp
- by, lul - la - by, lul - la - by.

5. DASHING AWAY WITH THE SMOOTHING IRON

Dash - ing a - way with the smooth-ing iron,
Dash - ing a - way with the smooth-ing iron, Ah
mp
Dash - ing a - way with the smooth-ing iron, Ah
mf
Dash-ing a - way with the smooth-ing iron,
mf
Dash-ing a - way with the smooth-ing iron,
f
Dash-ing a - way with the smooth-ing iron She stole my heart a - way.
dim.
f
Dash-ing a - way with the smooth-ing iron She stole my heart a - way.
dim.
f
Dash-ing a - way with the smooth-ing iron She stole my heart a - way.
dim.
f
Dash-ing a - way with the smooth-ing iron She stole, she stole my heart a -
dim.
mf
2. 'Twas
p
mp
She
p
mp
She
p
p
mp
- way. 2. 'Twas on a Tues - day morn - ing And there I saw my
on a Tues - day morn - ing And there I saw my dar - ling, She

looked so neat in ev - 'ry high de - gree,
looked so neat in ev - 'ry high de - gree,
dar - - ling,
looked so neat and charm - ing In ev - 'ry high de - gree, She
A - hang - ing out her lin - en O,
She looked so neat A - hang - ing out her lin - en O,
looked so neat and nim - ble O A - hang - ing out her lin - en O,
mf cresc.
Dash-ing a - way with the
mf
cresc.
Dash-ing a - way with the smooth - ing iron,
mf
cresc.
Dash-ing a - way with the smooth - ing iron, Dash-ing a - way,
(mf)
cresc.
Dash-ing a - way with the smooth - ing iron, Dash-ing a - way with the smooth - ing iron,

f
dim.
Dash-ing a - way with the smooth-ing iron She stole my heart a - way.
smooth - ing iron, the smooth-ing iron, She stole my heart a - way.
Dash-ing a - way with the smooth-ing iron She stole my heart a - way.
mf
Dash-ing a - way with the smooth-ing iron She stole my heart a - way. 3. 'Twas
Dash-ing a - way with the smooth-ing iron She stole my heart a - way.
p
mp
'Twas on Wed - n'sday
'Twas on Wed - n'sday
on a Wed - n'sday morn - ing And there I saw my dar - ling, She
'Twas on Wed - n'sday
A.
T.
Bar.
B.
morn - ing She looked so charm - ing,
morn - ing She looked so charm - ing,
looked so neat and charm - ing In ev - 'ry high de - gree. She
morn - ing She looked so charm - ing,

She looked so nim-ble starch-ing her lin - en O,
She looked so nim-ble starch-ing her lin - en O,
looked so neat and nim - ble O A - starch-ing of her lin - en O,
She looked so nim-ble starch-ing her lin - en O,
Dash - ing a - way, Dash - ing a - way,
Dash - ing a - way, Dash - ing a - way,
Dash-ing a - way with the smooth-ing iron, Dash-ing a - way with the smooth - ing iron,
Dash - ing a - way, dash - ing a - way,
S.
A.
T.
Bar.
B.
mf
f
4. 'Twas
Dash-ing a - way with the iron She stole my heart a - way. 4. 'Twas
Dash-ing a - way with the iron She stole my heart a - way. 4. 'Twas
Dash-ing a - way with the smooth-ing iron She stole my heart a - way. 4. 'Twas
Dash-ing a - way with the iron She stole my heart a - way. 4. 'Twas

on a Thurs-day morn - ing And there I saw my dar - ling, She
on a Thurs - day morn - ing And there I saw my dar - ling,
on a Thurs-day morn - ing And there I saw my dar - ling, She
on a Thurs-day morn - ing And there I saw my dar - ling, She
on a Thurs-day morn - ing And there I saw my dar - ling,
mf
looked so neat and charm - ing in ev - 'ry high de - gree, She
in ev - 'ry high de - gree, She
looked so neat and charm - ing in high de - gree, She
looked so neat and charm - ing in ev - 'ry high de - gree,
in high de - gree,
looked so neat and nim - ble O A - iron - ing of her lin - en O,
looked so neat and nim - ble O A - iron - ing of her lin - en O,
looked so neat and nim - ble O A - iron - ing of her lin - en O,
A - iron - ing of her lin - en O,
A - iron - ing of her lin - en O,

mp
Dash-ing a-way with the smooth-ing iron,
mf
Dash-ing a-way with the smooth-ing iron,
Dash-ing a-way with the smooth-ing iron,
f
Dash-ing a-way with the smooth-ing iron She stole my heart a-way.
dim.
p
Ah
mf dolce
5. 'Twas on a Fri-day morn-ing And there I saw my dar-ling, She looked so neat and charm-ing in
Ah
2

Ah
Ah
ev - 'ry high de - gree, She looked so neat and nim - ble O A - fold - ing of her
Ah
Ah
mp
Ah
mp
Ah
lin - en O, Dash-ing a - way with the smooth-ing iron, Dash-ing a - way with the smooth-ing iron,
mf
Ah
Dash-ing a - way with the smooth-ing iron,
mp
Ah
cresc.
f
She stole my heart a - way.
p leggiero
6. 'Twas
Dash-ing a - way with the smooth-ing iron She stole my heart a - way.
Dash-ing a - way with the smooth-ing iron She stole my heart a - way.

mp
on a Sat-ur-day morn - ing She looked so neat and
on a Sat-ur-day morn - ing She looked so neat and
on a Sat-ur-day morn - ing She looked so neat and
p
on And there I saw my dar - ling, She looked so neat and
p leggiero
And there I saw my dar - ling,
charm - ing in ev - 'ry high de - gree,
charm - ing in ev - 'ry high de - gree, She looked so neat and
charm - ing in ev - 'ry high de - gree,
charm - ing in ev - 'ry high de - gree, She looked so neat and
She looked so neat and
A - air - ing of her lin - en O, Dash-ing a - way with the
nim - ble O A - air - ing of her lin - en O,
A - air - ing of her lin - en O,
mf
nim - ble O Dash-ing a - way with the
nim - ble O Dash-ing a - way with the

smooth - ing iron, Dash-ing a - way with the smooth - ing iron, Dash-ing a - way with the
Dash-ing a - way with the smooth - ing iron, Dash-ing a - way with the
Dash-ing a - way with the smooth - ing iron, Dash-ing a - way with the
smooth - ing iron, Dash-ing a - way with the smooth - ing iron, Dash-ing a - way with the
smooth - ing iron, Dash-ing a - way with the smooth - ing iron, the
smooth-ing iron, She stole my heart a - way. Ding dong ding dong
smooth-ing iron, She stole my heart a - way. 7. 'Twas on a Sun - day morn - ing And
smooth-ing iron, She stole my heart a - way. Ding dong ding dong
smooth-ing iron, She stole my heart a - way. 7. 'Twas on a Sun - day morn - ing And
smooth-ing iron, She stole my heart a - way. Ding
ding dong ding dong, She looked so neat and charm - ing in ev - 'ry high de -
there I saw my dar - ling. Ah
ding dong ding dong, She looked so neat and charm - ing in ev - 'ry high de -
there I saw my dar - ling, Ah
dong Ah

Reproduced and printed by Halstan & Co. Ltd., Amersham, Bucks., England